Crayola SUMMER COLORS

Mari Schuh

Lerner Publications ◆ Minneapolis

TO FAIRMONT ELEMENTARY SCHOOL

Official Licensed Product
Lerner Publications Company
A division of Lerner Publishing Group, Inc.
241 First Avenue North
Minneapolis, MN 55401 USA

For reading levels and more information, look up this title at www.lernerbooks.com.

Main body text set in Billy Infant Regular 24/36.
Typeface provided by SparkyType.

Library of Congress Cataloging-in-Publication Data

Names: Schuh, Mari C., 1975–
Title: Crayola summer colors / by Mari Schuh.
Description: Minneapolis : Lerner Publications, [2018] | Series: Crayola seasons |
    Audience: Age 4-9. | Audience: K to grade 3. | Includes bibliographical references
    and index.
Identifiers: LCCN 2016046937 (print) | LCCN 2016048155 (ebook) | ISBN
    9781512432909 (lb : alk. paper) | ISBN 9781512455755 (pb : alk. paper) | ISBN
    9781512449310 (eb pdf)
Subjects: LCSH: Summer—Juvenile literature. | Seasons—Juvenile literature. |
    Crayons—Juvenile literature.
Classification: LCC QB637.6 .S378 2018 (print) | LCC QB637.6 (ebook) | DDC 535.6—
    dc23

LC record available at https://lccn.loc.gov/2016046937

Manufactured in the United States of America
1-41821-23781-1/24/2017

TABLE OF CONTENTS

SUMMER DAYS

The sun shines. The fresh grass is green, and the sky is bright blue.

4

FLOWERS AND FOOD

Pretty flowers grow in the summer sun.

Their green stems get taller.

Black-and-yellow bumblebees buzz around. They land on colorful flowers and sip nectar.

You can draw the bumblebee's fuzzy body. Start with many short lines.

How does it look?

Bright purple flowers grow in summer heat.

What color of flowers do you like best?

Juicy fruits and berries are ready to eat.

You can draw berries by placing lots of small circles close together.

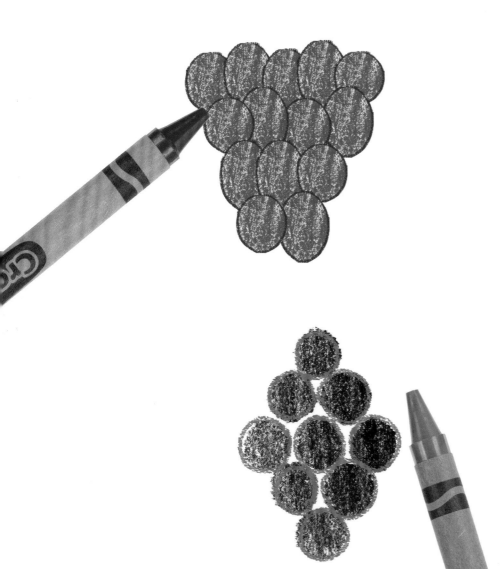

Draw your favorite berry, or create a new type of berry!

Sweet treats keep you cool on hot summer days.

Eat them before they melt!

What colors will you eat today?

SUMMER FUN

Fireworks and sparklers light up the sky. Celebrate the Fourth of July by waving a red, white, and blue flag!

Batter up!

A baseball team plays on a green field.
See the checkered design of the mowed grass on the field?

You can make a checkered design by overlapping thin and wide lines.

See how the lines make squares?

Summer is full of fun and games.

What colors do
you see in summer?

WORLD OF COLORS

Summer is so colorful! Here are some Crayola® crayon colors used in this book. Can you find them in the photos? What colors do you see in summer?

CERISE

VIVID TANGERINE

SKY BLUE

RAZZMATAZZ

SUNSET ORANGE

CERULEAN

WILD WATERMELON

CARIBBEAN GREEN

DENIM

RED

GREEN

VIVID VIOLET

YELLOW

AQUAMARINE

FUCHSIA

GLOSSARY

checkered: a pattern of squares that alternates between two colors or shades

firework: a device that is loud and colorful when it is burned or exploded. Fireworks are used at celebrations.

nectar: a sweet liquid found in many flowers

sparkler: a type of firework that you hold in your hand and that lets off bright sparks as it burns

stem: the thin part of a plant from which the leaves and flowers grow

TO LEARN MORE

BOOKS

Lindeen, Mary. *Summer*. Chicago: Norwood House, 2015. Learn about all the fun activities that happen in summer.

Moon, Walt K. *Summer Is Fun!* Minneapolis: Lerner Publications, 2017. Learn about what happens in summer.

Murray, Julie. *Summer*. Minneapolis: Abdo Kids, 2016. Discover the weather and activities of the summer season.

WEBSITES

Cardboard Tube Fireworks
http://www.crayola.com/crafts/cardboard-tube -fireworks-craft/
Celebrate the Fourth of July by using a recycled cardboard tube to paint patriotic fireworks.

Summer Word Search
http://www.sciencekids.co.nz/quizzes/wordsearch /summer.html
Find words about summer in this fun word search. Can you find the word *sun*? Do you see the word *hot*?

PHOTO ACKNOWLEDGMENTS

The images in this book are used with the permission of: © Philip James Corwin/ Getty Images, p. 1; © Elena Yakusheva/Shutterstock.com, p. 2; © Serrnovik/ Dreamstime.com, pp. 4-5; © Aleksey Ipatov/Dreamstime.com, pp. 6-7; © Maite Lohmann/Dreamstime.com, p. 8; © Lucian Coman/Shutterstock.com, pp. 10-11; © iStockphoto.com/mjostodd, p. 12; © Mike Kemp/Getty Images, p. 14; Ariel Skelley Blend Images/Newscom, pp. 16-17; © Macduff Everton/Getty Images, p. 18; © NadyaEugene/Shutterstock.com, pp. 20-21.

Cover: © Buntoon Rodseng/Shutterstock.com (beach chairs); © Elena Shashkina/ Shutterstock.com (sandy beach background).

LERNER
e
SOURCE™

Expand learning beyond the printed book. Download free, complementary educational resources for this book from our website, www.lerneresource.com.